THE POWER OF FAITH
Putting your faith into action

DR. J.L. WILLIAMS

Copyright © 2017 by Dr. J.L. Williams

The Power of Faith
Putting your faith into action
by Dr. J.L. Williams

Printed in the United States of America.

Edited by Xulon Press.

ISBN 9781498499156

All rights reserved solely by the author. The author guarantees all contents are original and do not infringe upon the legal rights of any other person or work. No part of this book may be reproduced in any form without the permission of the author. The views expressed in this book are not necessarily those of the publisher.

Unless otherwise indicated, Scripture quotations taken from the King James Version (KJV) – *public domain.*

www.xulonpress.com

PREFACE

This is part two of a four-part series titled,
"The Power Series."

DEDICATION

This book is dedicated to those whose faith may have wavered. May this book bring you to experience complete trust once again, because within you resides the *Power of Faith*.

DEFINITIONS

Power: the ability or capacity to act or perform effectively.

Faith: complete trust.

THE POWER OF FAITH

Dear friend in Christ:

Greetings in the name of our Lord and Savior, Jesus Christ. Today, we are going to speak on an important and crucial subject. It is an important element in your relationship with Jesus Christ. It is the subject of "faith." It is an important key in your walk with the Lord. In Hebrews 11:1, it says, "Now faith is the substance [the assurance, confirmation, the title deed] of things hoped for, the evidence of things not seen." Faith is the confirmation of things hoped for. In other words, something that we are believing for, or hoping for. "The evidence of things not seen" means we do not see the evidence, or results, but we know what we believed or hoped for will come to pass.

Here are some men and women of faith in the Bible: Sarah, Abel, Enoch, Noah, Abraham, Isaac, Jacob, Joseph, Moses, and Rahab. St. Matthew 9:22 states, "But Jesus turned him about, and when he saw her, he said, 'Daughter, be of good comfort; thy faith hath made thee whole.' And the woman was made whole from that hour." This was the woman who had the issue of blood for twelve years.

She had spent all her money on earthly doctors, who did her no good. As a matter of fact, she did not get better, but instead, her sickness got worse. She said within herself (faith kicked in) if she could touch the hem of Christ's garment, she would be made whole. When you exhibit faith in God, it pleases Him, and He will answer your prayers. The woman's faith, which included not only her confidence in Christ's restorative power, but her importunate initiative as an unclean woman (Leviticus 15:19) occasions her healing.

St. Matthew 9:29 states, "Then touched he their eyes, saying, 'According to your faith be it unto you.'" This is the story of two blind men who came to Jesus to receive their sight. Jesus asked them a question in verse 28, "'Believe ye that I am able to do this?' They said unto him, 'Yea Lord.'" We must believe God will answer our petitions; we must believe He can and will do what He said. That is faith. The Bible says the two blind men received their sight. They received, because they believed. If we today believe God, we too will receive (faith).

St. Mark 2:5 states, "When Jesus saw their faith, he said unto the sick of the palsy, 'Son, thy sins be forgiven thee.'" The response of Jesus reflects the Jewish view that forgiveness of sins must precede physical healing. Whether or not this particular disease was the consequence of sin, Jesus went to the heart of the matter. Sin and disease are effects of evil, and Jesus reveals God's opposition to evil in any way it may manifest. His goal is to bring complete wholeness to people. Before we are healed of a physical ailment, we first must be healed of our sins. The spiritual must be dealt with first, then the physical man. Remember, first spiritual, then physical. Because God is holy, and sin cannot stand in His presence, it must be done away

The Power of Faith

with. That's why the blood of Jesus wipes our slate clean, and we can stand before God, pure and clean, covered by the blood of Jesus! Hallelujah!

St. Mark 4:40 states, "And he (Jesus) said unto them, 'Why are ye so fearful? How is it that ye have no faith?'" The disciples were afraid or fearful of the storm and when you exhibit fear, which means false evidence appears real; you have no faith. Fear is the opposing force to faith. So when Christ comes, and the storms of life begin to beat upon our lives, remember, the Master is on board, and you have to call Him and He will calm the storms and the crises in your life. You must have faith in Him, and do not fear.

St. Mark 11:22 states, "And Jesus answering saith unto them, 'Have faith in God.'" Jesus said, "Have faith in God." Or it translates another way, "Have the faith of God." Faith is the key that releases the resources of heaven into our situation. So, "have faith in God."

St. Luke 7:9 states, "When Jesus heard these things, he marveled at him, and turned him about, and said unto the people that followed him, 'I say unto you, I have not found so great faith, no, not in Israel.'" This is the story of the centurion's servant being healed by Jesus. The great faith of the gentile centurion is the key to the passage, "great faith" being explained as the centurion's understanding and response to an authoritative word from Jesus (verses 7 and 8). His faith stands in stark contrast to the curious doubt in Israel.

St. Luke 7:50 states, "And he [Jesus] said to the woman, 'Thy faith hath saved thee; go in peace.'" This is the story of Jesus forgiving a sinful woman. Faith secured her pardon, and the realization of God's forgiveness brought forth her expression of gratitude. "Save" is the word *sozo* in Greek, and it means "to save, heal, cure, preserve, keep safe and sound, rescue from danger or destruction, deliver." *Sozo* saves from physical death by healing, and from spiritual death by forgiving sin and its effects.

St. Luke 17:5-6 states, "And the apostles said unto the Lord, 'Increase our faith.' And the Lord said, 'If ye had faith as a grain of mustard seed, ye might say unto this sycamore tree, be thou plucked up by the root, and be thou planted in the sea; and it should obey you.'" The apostles or disciples felt the need for greater faith to meet the standard Jesus demanded; the amount of faith is not as important as its quality. We must increase our faith, and the way we increase our faith is through the hearing of the Word of God.

Romans 10:17 states, "So then faith cometh by hearing, and hearing by the Word of God." One can only have faith through the hearing of the Word of God! Faith will come as we hear the Word of God. Faith comes not by hearing things of the world, or by denominational doctrines, or by our ideas, or watching perverse things on television, or partying. Faith comes through hearing the Word of God.

Romans 12:3 states, "For I say, through the grace given unto me, to every man that is among you, not to think of himself more highly than he ought to think; but to think soberly, according as God hath dealt to every man the measure of faith." The apostle Paul says we are not to think too highly of ourselves than we ought to. However, we are to think soberly, according as God hath dealt to every man the measure of faith. All men have faith, because God has given all men a measure of faith, and in order to increase our faith, we must exercise it.

Romans 14:23 states, "And he that doubted is damned if he eat, because he eateth not of faith: for whatsoever is not of faith is sin." Do not place yourself in condemnation about what you eat, or whether or not you eat meat. Do not let others place you in condemnation. Anything not of faith is sin. Doubting is not faith. Therefore, doubting is sin.

Second Corinthians 5:7 states, "For we walk by faith, not by sight." This is how the Christian should walk, live, and talk; everything should be done by faith, not by sight, because if you see the thing, it is not faith. Faith is something you do not see, yet you believe. Lord, help your children to walk by faith, not by sight.

Galatians 3:11 states, "But that no man is justified by the law in the sight of God, it is evident: for the just shall live by faith." In the sight of God, the law justifies no man. For the law was a schoolmaster, telling us what was wrong, and it was quite impossible to keep the law, because if you broke the law in one area, you were guilty of breaking all of them. Thank God for grace, and we who are under the dispensation of grace must and shall live by faith.

Ephesians 2:8-9 states, "For by grace are ye saved through faith; and that not of yourselves: it is the gift of God. Not of works, lest any man should boast." We are saved by the grace of God through faith, and we did not do this on our own, but it is the gift of God (grace), and it is not granted by works. We cannot work to obtain salvation. Yet, it is the gift of God, and because it is a gift of God, you and I cannot boast about it. We cannot say it was because of my good works, or my standing in the community, or my charities that I contribute to, or my tithes and offerings, or my religious prayers, or my good morals. All of our righteousness is a filthy rag before God. We cannot and we dare not boast in ourselves, or in anything or anyone else except the Lord Jesus Christ, who made it all possible for us to have this great salvation.

Ephesians 6:16 states, "Above all, taking the shield of faith, wherewith ye shall be able to quench all the fiery darts of the wicked." You see how important faith is? The Word says, "Above all, take the shield of faith!" With the shield of faith we shall—not hope, not guess, but we *shall*—be able to quench or extinguish, and put out all of the fiery darts of the wicked one. The devil will shoot his darts of fear, doubt, unbelief, and worry to hinder our faith, to injure our faith, to damage our faith in God. Thanks be to God. The devil cannot hurt us when we, above all, take the shield of faith. Faith will give us the victory over the devil. Glory! Hallelujah! Thank you, Jesus!

Colossians 1:23 states, "If ye continue in the faith grounded and settled, and be not moved away from the hope of the gospel, which ye have heard, and which was preached to every creature which is under heaven; whereof I Paul am made a minister." Paul is speaking to the saints and the faithful brethren in Christ, and he is speaking to us today, telling us to continue in the faith, and not only to continue in the faith, but he says we must be grounded and settled. In other words, we must be rooted in the Word of God. We must have our faith rooted deep, anchored in the bedrock of God's eternal Word, and not be moved away from the hope of the gospel. The devil will try to uproot you, to make you unsettled. You must have enduring faith so the devil cannot take away the hope you have in the Lord.

First Timothy 6:12 states, "Fight the good fight of faith, lay hold on eternal life, where unto thou art also called, and has professed a good profession before many witnesses." Paul encourages and exhorts his spiritual son, Timothy, to fight the good fight of faith, and to lay hold on eternal life. We must realize we are in a fight. A war. However, we are not fighting naturally, in the physical realm (flesh), but we are fighting, warring in the spiritual realm, and we must make sure we are armed with the spiritual warfare and equipment to fight the good fight of faith.

Hebrews 12:2 states, "Looking unto Jesus, the author and finisher of our faith: who for the joy that was set before him endured the cross, despising the shame, and is set down at the right hand of the throne of God." When it comes to our faith, we must look to only one person. Not your earthly father, or earthly mother, not sisters or brothers, not friends or acquaintances. We must look to the beginner and completer of our faith. We must look to the starter and the ender of our faith. We must look to Jesus. The author and finisher of our faith. What He starts with you and inside you, He will finish it. Jesus never leaves a task halfway done, but He finishes everything to the last detail. That's why Jesus said, "Before one jot or tittle of my words shall pass, heaven and earth shall pass" (St. Matthew 5:18).

James 2:20 states, "But wilt thou know, O vain man, that faith without works is dead?" The apostle James is simply saying faith and works go together in the sense of showing you are indeed the person who has faith, because your works will complement your faith. Your faith will produce action. You will not only talk faith, but you will live faith out in your daily life. I'm glad for faith. We must have faith, because we cannot please God without faith. So I pray that faith will begin to grow inside of you right now so you will be a great Christian who exhibits great faith in the Lord! God bless you!

Dear friend, please listen to me:
You may not believe the sky is blue, but it is!
You may not believe fire burns, but it does!
You may not believe you will die one day, but you will!
You may not believe after death comes the judgment, but it does!
You may not believe one day you will stand before a holy, righteous God, and give an account for your life, but you will!
So I plead with you to accept Jesus Christ into your heart, and make Him your savior and Lord of your life, before it is too late.
Eternity is too long of a time to be separated from the Lord Jesus Christ!

Now may the blessing of God's Word be upon you, blessing you in all spiritual knowledge, wisdom, and the enlightenment of your understanding, so His Word will stand sure in your heart, and be applied to your everyday Christian living. Amen.

AUTHOR'S BIOGRAPHY

Dr. J. L. Williams is an associate minister at the New Zion M. B. Church of Clearwater, Florida, where Dr. LeRoy Howard is pastor. Dr. Williams is the author of the following books: *Messages of Inspiration Volumes I and II*, and *The Power of Choice*.

www.ingramcontent.com/pod-product-compliance
Lightning Source LLC
LaVergne TN
LVHW021751060526
838200LV00052B/3580